HISTORY'S GREATEST WARRIORS

Ninja

by Sean McDaniel

BELLWETHER MEDIA • MINNEAPOLIS, MN

TM

Are you ready to take it to the extreme?
Torque books thrust you into the action-packed world
of sports, vehicles, mystery, and adventure. These books
may include dirt, smoke, fire, and dangerous stunts.
Warning: read at your own risk.

Library of Congress Cataloging-in-Publication Data

McDaniel, Sean.
 Ninja / by Sean McDaniel.
     p. cm. -- (Torque : History's greatest warriors)
 Includes bibliographical references and index.
 Summary: "Engaging images accompany information about ninja. The combination of high-interest
subject matter and light text is intended for students in grades 3 through 7"--Provided by publisher.
 ISBN 978-1-60014-630-5 (hardcover : alk. paper)
 1. Ninja--Juvenile literature. 2. Ninjutsu--Juvenile literature. I. Title.
 UB271.J3M44 2012
 355.5'48--dc22   2011003070

This edition first published in 2012 by Bellwether Media, Inc.

Printed in the United States of America, North Mankato, MN.

080111   1187

Contents

What Are Ninja?

Hundreds of years ago, Japan was a place of violence and war. Great armies battled for land and power. However, not all fights happened on a battlefield. Some fights involved secret agents known as ninja. Army leaders hired these masters of **stealth** and **martial arts** to attack the enemy by surprise.

Ninja performed many missions. They were sent to **infiltrate** enemy forces. Some focused on **sabotage**. They set off explosives in enemy territory or burned down buildings. Others served as **assassins**.

The earliest reports of ninja date back to the 1100s. The first ninja came from two areas of Japan called Iga and Koga. They were very different from the powerful **samurai** who led the Japanese armies. Samurai came from rich families. Ninja were usually common people. Samurai valued honor and many thought the secret ways of the ninja were dishonorable.

samurai

Ninja Fact

The secret ways of the ninja led to many legends. People spread stories that ninja could control nature, walk on water, and become invisible.

Ninja Training

People who wanted to become ninja
had to master many skills. The martial arts
and **tactics** of ninja were called *ninjutsu*.
Ninja learned how to use stealth and
disguise to spy on enemies. They practiced
using poison, explosives, and other
weapons. *Ninjutsu* focused on strength,
speed, and **stamina**. Ninja needed to be
in excellent physical shape.

The Nakagawa-Ryu was a school started by expert ninja Nakagawa Shoshujin. He trained 10 to 20 young ninja at a time. He taught them to be excellent spies.

Survival skills were also important to learn. Ninja often worked alone for many months. They had to be able to find food, build fires, and **purify** water in the wild. They also needed to know how to swim, ride a horse, read, and write. These skills were important for traveling and communication.

Ninja Roles

Ninja carried out several different kinds of missions. Their training helped prepare them for these roles:

✳ ## Spies (*kancho*)

Spies infiltrated enemy territory. They used disguise to blend in and collect information about the enemy.

✳ ## Scouts (*teisatsu*)

These ninja watched the enemy from the outside. They gathered information about enemy buildings, passwords, and guards.

✳ ## Agitators (*koran*)

Agitators were skilled in sabotage. They often set fire to castles or enemy camps.

✳ ## Surprise attackers (*kisho*)

These ninja often carried out assassinations. They sometimes killed people while they were sleeping.

Ninja Weapons and Gear

shuriken

Ninja were armed with many weapons. The long, curved *katana* was their main sword. Ninja also carried *shuriken* to throw at enemies. *Shuriken* were small weapons with pointed blades. The *tekken* was a claw-like device worn on the hand of a ninja. It could be used to fight or climb. Small saws called *shikoro ken* were often used to cut through wooden walls and sneak into buildings.

katana

Ninja needed other gear as well. *Kaginawa* were long ropes that ended in hooks. Ninja used them to climb walls. The *saoto hikigane* was a listening tool. Ninja placed this tube on a wall to hear what was happening on the other side.

kaginawa

Ninja Fact

The *kusarigama* was a very deadly weapon. It had a handle with a blade at one end and a chain at the other. An iron weight was connected to the end of the chain.

Ninja clothing allowed for swift and silent movement. Ninja wore loose pants and a shirt with a belt. A wrap called a cowl covered a ninja's head and face. Only the eyes were visible. Ninja wore socks called *tabi* on their feet. They often wore sandals if the ground was rough.

The Decline of the Ninja

Oda Nobunaga

The ninja were most powerful in Japan from 1467 to 1649. This period was called the Age of Warring States. Skilled ninja were in great demand. However, they were also feared. In the late 1500s, a **daimyo** named Oda Nobunaga rose to power. He wanted to **unify** Japan and did not trust the ninja. He attacked Iga and many ninja were killed.

Shimabara Castle

Ninja Fact

The last war that ninja fought in was the Shimabara Rebellion from 1637 to 1638. The ninja helped carry out secret raids on the enemy castle. The raids helped their side win the battle.

Some ninja fled Iga. Others fought against Nobunaga for other daimyo. However, Nobunaga's side eventually won. Japan became unified under one ruler. Ninja were no longer needed. Slowly, the ways of the ninja faded. Today, only their legend remains.

Glossary

assassins—people who kill others for political or military reasons; assassins are often hired by someone to kill another person.

daimyo—a lord, or landowner, during the Age of Warring States

disguise—clothing worn to hide one's true identity

infiltrate—to secretly join a group to spy on it

martial arts—styles of fighting and self-defense that involve precise body movements

purify—to make water safe to drink by removing harmful materials

sabotage—actions that destroy property or hinder military operations

samurai—skilled warriors who led Japanese armies during the Age of Warring States

stamina—the ability to stay active; ninja trained to have a lot of stamina.

stealth—quiet movement that is difficult to detect

tactics—strategies for moving and attacking; ninja tactics involved stealth and surprise.

unify—to bring together as one

To Learn More

AT THE LIBRARY

Devin, John. *Samurai*. Minneapolis, Minn.:
Bellwether Media, 2012.

Doeden, Matt. *Life as a Ninja: An Interactive History Adventure*. Mankato, Minn.: Capstone Press, 2010.

Guillain, Charlotte. *Ninja*. Chicago, Ill.:
Raintree, 2010.

ON THE WEB

Learning more about ninja
is as easy as 1, 2, 3.

1. Go to www.factsurfer.com.

2. Enter "ninja" into the search box.

3. Click the "Surf" button and you will see a list of related Web sites.

With factsurfer.com, finding more information
is just a click away.

WWW.FACTSURFER.COM

Index